CONFIDENT

Titles in this Series:

Afraid	Happy
Angry	Hurt
Brave	Jealous
Confident	Lonely
Friendly	Sad

Copyright © text 1994 Steck-Vaughn Company

Library of Congress Cataloging-in-Publication Data
(Revised for vols. 7, 8, 9, 10)
Amos, Janine.
      Feelings.
      Contents: [7] Brave – [8] Confident –
[9] Friendly – [10] Happy
      1. Emotions–Case studies–Juvenile
literature. [1. Emotions. 2. Conduct of
life.] I. Green, Gwen, ill. II. Title.
BF561.A515 1994   152.4   90-46540
ISBN 0-8172-3775-5 (v. 1)
Originally ISBN listed as 0-8172-3775-5
      Afraid ISBN 0-8172-3775-5 (v. 1): Angry ISBN 0-8172-3776-3 (v.2);
Hurt ISBN 0-8172-3777-1 (v. 3); Jealous ISBN 0-8172-3778-X (v. 4);
Lonely ISBN 0-8172-3779-8 (v. 5); Sad ISBN 0-8172-3780-1 (v. 6)

New titles are listed as: Brave ISBN 0-8114-9228-1 (v. 7); Confident
ISBN 0-8114-9229-X (v. 8); Friendly ISBN 0-8114-9230-3 (v. 9); Happy
ISBN 0-8114-9231-1 (v. 10)

Editor: Deborah Biber
Electronic production: Alan Haimowitz
Printed in Spain
Bound in the United States
1 2 3 4 5 6 7 8 9 0 LB 98 97 96 95 94 93

CONFIDENT

By Janine Amos
Illustrated by Gwen Green

RSVP
RAINTREE
STECK-VAUGHN
PUBLISHERS
The Steck-Vaughn Company

Austin, Texas

KEVIN'S STORY

Kevin looked at his spelling words. Not one was right. He covered the page with his arm. Kevin didn't like spelling or reading or math. He didn't like school. Everyone else went so fast.

Kevin got out his felt pens. He started a small drawing at the very bottom of the page. He liked drawing—not the kind they did in art class. Kevin's houses and trees always looked funny. But Kevin did like drawing dinosaurs. He'd copied lots of them from his brother's book. Now he could do them right out of his head.

Kevin's dinosaur got bigger. It was green and scaly. He gave it yellow eyes and a long tail. It went right over the spelling words.

"Are you listening, Kevin?" said a voice. Kevin jumped. It was his teacher, Mrs. Blake.

"We're going to start on some projects," said Mrs. Blake. "You can work in teams. Each table will be a team and do a different project."

Kevin's group waited to find out what their project would be.

"I hope it's soccer!" said Ben. "I know lots about that."

"I could write a poem," said José. "A soccer poem!"

"I don't know much about anything," thought Kevin. He colored in his dinosaur very slowly. He tried not to think about the project.

Why doesn't Kevin want to think about the project?

Mrs. Blake reached Kevin's table. "Your project's about Monsters," she said.

"Great!" shouted Ben. "I'll write about a moon monster."

"You can do stories, poems, pictures, facts—anything you like about monsters," said Mrs. Blake. "Then we'll put them all together to make a book."

Kevin's group started work. Kevin watched them. "I can't do this," he thought.

Ben looked at Kevin's empty page. "Hurry up, or you won't be in the Monster book," said Ben.

"It's stupid, anyway," said Kevin. But he picked up his pen.

Does Kevin really think the book is stupid?

Kevin was scared to start. He looked at everyone else. Some children had asked for extra paper.

Mrs. Blake came back to Kevin's table.

"Do you need some help getting started?" she asked.

"I can't do anything," said Kevin sadly.

"You can," said Mrs. Blake. "Why don't you do a picture with your new felt pens?"

Kevin sighed.

"I think you'll do a terrific picture," said Mrs. Blake. "Come on, give it a try!"

"OK," said Kevin. Then he had an idea.

Can you guess Kevin's idea?

"Do dinosaurs count as monsters?" Kevin asked his teacher. He said it very quietly, just in case it was silly.

"Yes," said Mrs. Blake. She smiled. "What a good idea!"

Kevin grinned. He got out his green felt pen. Soon he had covered the paper with the shape of a huge dinosaur. Then, very carefully, he started to color it in.

Kevin's tongue stuck out as he worked. He was thinking hard.

"This will be the best dinosaur I've ever done," he thought.

At the end of the lesson Mrs. Blake collected the work. Kevin put his dinosaur on the Monster pile.

"That's a great picture!" said José. The others crowded around.

"Can that be the cover of our Monster book?" Ben asked Mrs. Blake.

"You'll have to ask Kevin," said Mrs. Blake.

"OK," said Kevin, smiling.

How do you think Kevin feels now?

Feeling like Kevin

Kevin didn't find school work easy. Other children worked faster than he did. Kevin felt a little different. He felt he couldn't do anything well. He got so used to this feeling that he almost stopped trying. He lost confidence in himself.

Feeling confident

Feeling confident is about believing in yourself. It's about feeling brave and strong inside. If you're confident, you'll try out new things. You'll believe you can do them.

Never give up!

When lots of things go wrong for you, it's easy to feel like Kevin. You might get scared to try again. Then it's good to remind yourself of what you *can* do well—just as Kevin remembered his dinosaurs. You might be a good swimmer, a good helper, or a good friend. Everyone's good at something.

Think about it

Read the stories in this book. Think about the people in them. Do you feel like them sometimes? Think what makes you feel confident.

ALLISON'S STORY

Chorus had just finished. It would soon be time for the final concert. Allison was looking forward to that.

"I know all the songs now," she thought, as she pulled on her coat.

Just then Mr. James came over. He was in charge of the chorus.

"I've been thinking, Allison," said Mr. James. "Would you like a part in the school play?"

Allison didn't know what to say.

"I mean instead of the chorus," Mr. James went on.

Some other girls were listening. Now they joined in.

"You sing too loud, Allison," said one girl.

"You can't hit the right notes," said a small girl with bushy hair. Allison turned red. She looked at Mr. James.

The teacher smiled at Allison. He held out a sheet of paper.

"Here are the words for one part in the play. Could you look at them at home? Then during our break tomorrow we can go through them," he said.

Allison nodded. The girl with the bushy hair giggled. Mr. James gave the girl a cross look.

"You have a clear reading voice," he told Allison loudly. "The play needs someone like you."

Allison stuffed the piece of paper into her pocket. She was trying hard not to cry.

Why was Allison upset? How would you feel if you were Allison?

Allison ran home. She told her mom and dad what had happened.

"I know all the songs, and now I'm not even in the chorus," she said sadly. "I must be really bad at singing."

Allison's dad looked at her carefully. He turned off the television.

"What part has Mr. James asked you to learn for the play, Allison?" he asked.

Allison handed her dad the piece of paper.

"It's the part of the Narrator," said Allison's dad. "Do you know what that is?"

"I don't care," said Allison quietly.

"It's the storyteller," said Allison's mom. "That's an important part. The Narrator tells everyone what's happening as the play goes along."

"Why don't you read it, Allison?" said her dad. "Go on, try it out on us!"

"No," said Allison. "I won't be any good. I wasn't any good in the chorus, and I won't be any good in the play either."

Allison's dad frowned. "That's silly," he said. "We can't be good at everything. But we have to give ourselves a chance."

"I won't like acting as much as singing," said Allison.

"You might like it even more!" said her mom.

Do you think Allison's mom and dad are right?

Allison stood in the middle of the room. She read the words aloud to her mom and dad. She got some words a little muddled. But she managed to read it all. When Allison had finished, her mom and dad clapped.

"You were great!" they said together.

Allison smiled.

How do you think Allison is feeling now?

"It's long," said Allison, looking at all the writing. "I'll never remember all that!"

"Of course you will," said Allison's dad.

"I was too quiet, wasn't I?" asked Allison.

"You just need some practice," said her mom.

Allison practiced her part all evening. By bedtime she knew nearly all the words. So did her mom and dad!

"I bet I mess up tomorrow, with Mr. James," said Allison.

"You won't," said her dad. "Before you start, take a deep breath. Tell yourself you'll be great."

The next day Mr. James was waiting for Allison. "Would you like to read the part to me?" he asked.

Allison nodded. She felt a little worried.

Then Allison remembered what her dad had said. She took a deep breath and started to read.

When Allison finished, Mr. James clapped for ages.

"You were great!" he said. Allison was pleased.

"Are you still upset about the chorus?" asked Mr. James.

"I like singing," said Allison. "But acting's even better!"

How did Allison's mom and dad help?
Is Allison feeling confident now?

Feeling like Allison

Mr. James made Allison feel unsure about what she could do. So did the other girls. Allison lost confidence. But her mom and dad helped her to try again. And they helped her to practice. That made her feel more sure of herself.

Talking about it

When you're feeling like Allison, it's a good idea to talk about it. Tell an adult you trust. Ask the person to help you feel confident again. If you want to practice something, ask the adult to watch or listen. Remember, no one's good at everything. Try something new! Always practice so that you're ready. Then take a deep breath. Say to yourself, "I can do it!"

TOM'S STORY

"Oops!" Tom squeezed the toothpaste tube too hard. White paste hit the bathroom mirror. Tom dabbed at it with his washcloth. He was excited. Today the whole family was going on a picnic. They were taking Tom's friend Brian too.

Tom began to whistle. His whistling was not the best, but it was loud.

"Tom! Hurry up!" called his mom. "Brian's here."

"Coming!" shouted Tom. He ran into his room to find something to wear. Tom saw a T-shirt lying on the floor. He pulled it over his head.

"I love picnics!" thought Tom.

Tom was happy to see his friend.

"Hi, Brian. Let's pack the car!" he shouted.

"Oh no you don't," said Tom's mom. "Go straight back upstairs and put on a clean T-shirt. Why are you always so scruffy, Tom?" Tom turned red.

"Sorry," he said.

How do you think Tom is feeling now?

When Tom had changed, he helped to pack the car.

"Hey! Careful with my camera, Tom!" shouted his sister Dawn. "You'll break it!"

"I thought cameras were supposed to go snap!" said Tom smiling. But he put the camera down very carefully.

When they got out in the country, Tom's mom parked the car. Tom helped his dad to lay a tablecloth on the ground for the picnic.

"Look!" whispered Brian. It was a squirrel. Everyone watched it. Then Tom moved his foot, the leaves crackled—and the squirrel ran off. Tom felt awful.

"Leave it to you, Tom!" said his dad. That made Tom feel even worse.

Tom's dad got out the food. There was bread, meat, cheese, tomatoes, and Tom's favorite potato salad.

"Try some, it's great!" said Tom to Brian. Tom passed the cheese and put his elbow in the potato salad.

"Here we go again!" groaned Tom's mom. "Calm down, Tom."

"Sorry, Mom," said Tom. He sighed.

"Brian doesn't make mistakes all the time," thought Tom. "I wish I was Brian."

The next day Tom didn't whistle in the bathroom. He was on time for all his meals. And he was very quiet.

"Are you feeling OK, Tom?" asked his dad.

In the afternoon, Tom, Dawn, and their mom played hearts. Tom was careful to keep the cards in neat piles. He didn't shout or get excited.

"That wasn't much fun," said Dawn.

"Are you ill, Tom?" asked his mom.

"Tell us a joke," said his dad. But Tom couldn't think of a single one.

Do you think Tom's ill? What's wrong with him?

All day Tom was careful to get things right. But just before bedtime he poured some milk. Tom tripped—and the milk went everywhere! Tom shut his eyes.

"Oh, no!" he groaned. But nobody shouted at him.

When Tom opened his eyes, his mom, his dad, and Dawn were all watching him. They were smiling.

"That was a real milk shake," said Tom quietly.

"Yea!" said everyone else together.

As Tom got into bed that night, his mom gave him a hug.

"I'm sorry if we upset you at the picnic," she said.

"I tried to be like Brian today," said Tom. "But it didn't work."

"We didn't expect you to change," said Tom's mom.

"Things just happen when I'm around," said Tom.

"I know," said his mom, laughing. "But we like you just the way you are."

"Even my jokes?" asked Tom.

"Especially your jokes!" said his mom.

Feeling like Tom

Have you ever felt like Tom? Have you ever made mistakes and stopped liking yourself? It's not a good feeling, is it? You feel your confidence slipping away.

Being yourself

Tom learned that you can't be someone else. He found out something else, too. Tom learned that his family loved him for himself—even if he did make mistakes. Your friends and family feel the same way about you. They may not like everything you do—but they still like *you* !

Liking yourself

Tom was messy and he dropped things. But he was also helpful and funny. Like Tom, we all have parts that we'd like to change. But there are lots of good things about each of us, too. What do you like about yourself? What do your friends like about you? Liking yourself can help you to feel confident.

Feeling confident

Think about the stories in this book. Kevin, Allison, and Tom all had problems with feeling confident. They were all helped by other people to feel good about themselves. They helped themselves, too. Who could help you to become more confident? Can you help other people with their confidence—your sister, your brother, your friend?

If you are feeling frightened or unhappy, don't keep it to yourself. Talk to an adult you can trust:

- one of your parents or other relatives
- a friend's parent or other relative
- a teacher
- the principal
- someone else at school
- a neighbor
- someone at a church, temple, or synagogue

You can also find someone to talk to about a problem by calling places called "hotlines." One hotline is **Child Help**, which you can call from anywhere in the United States. Just call

1-800-422-4453

from any telephone and stay on the line. You don't need money to call.

Or look in the phone book to find another phone number of people who can help. Try

- Children and Family Service
- Family Service

Remember you can always call the Operator in any emergency. Just dial 0 or press the button that says 0 on the telephone.